# COVER TO COVER

# Prepared
## for Purpose

**EMPOWERED BY THE SPIRIT**

**CWR**

Trevor J. Partridge

# Contents

# Introduction

We commence our journey over the next six weeks of Lent, exploring the subject of being *Prepared for Purpose – Empowered by the Spirit*. Lent represents the forty days Jesus spent in the wilderness, where His humanity was fully put under the spotlight. The devil came and sorely tempted and tested Him to the limit. He was 'in all points tested as we are, yet without sin' (Heb. 4:15, NKJV).

The temptation is one of the most striking episodes in the life of our Lord. It was a full scrutiny of His humanity. He underwent a threefold trial, and it is important for us to understand the significance of the work of the Holy Spirit in this process. A failure to understand the work of the Holy Spirit in *our* lives when we face severe tests and trials, only ends in defeat, discouragement and disappointment.

Many think that Jesus carried out His powerful work because He was the Son of God. They think that it was His divinity which enabled His extraordinary earthly ministry; that He ministered out of His Deity rather than in His humanity.

However, Paul, in his letter to the church at Philippi, points out that Jesus willingly divested Himself of the glory of heaven, taking on in His birth the full likeness of man, that 'being in very nature God, [He] did not consider equality with God something to be grasped, but made himself nothing, taking the very nature of a servant, being made in human likeness. And being found in appearance as a man, he humbled himself and became obedient to death – even death on a cross!' (Phil. 2:6–8). Christ willingly gave up His right to express the power of His Deity while here on earth, subjecting Himself to the limitations of our humanity (John 1:1–2,14). Jesus' experience in the flesh was exactly like that of every other man (Heb. 2:17). Jesus testified of His own humanity: 'By myself I can do nothing' (John 5:30).

The forty days involved waiting, fasting and praying. The abstinence from food tested His humanity to its limits. He underwent this period not in His power as God – that had been willingly laid aside – but as a human being, enduring it just as you or I would, no different. He fasted – why fast? It is almost a forgotten practice today; the only fast most people seem to know about is 'fast food'. Fasting is subduing our natural appetite for food by a period of abstinence, in order to focus on deepening our spiritual relationship with God, letting the hunger pangs concentrate our mind on more eternal things. It was at this point in Jesus' fast that the devil sought to take advantage through temptation.

The wilderness in Scripture signifies a place and period of preparation for service and ministry. Prior to the forty days spent in the wilderness, Jesus performed no miracles and fulfilled no ministry. A closer look reveals the dimension of the Holy Spirit coming upon Him to endue Him with power and purpose, '... how God anointed Jesus of Nazareth with the Holy Spirit and with power, who went about doing good and healing all who were oppressed by the devil, for God was with him' (Acts 10:38, NKJV). It was the fullness of the Holy Spirit that empowered Him for ministry. Jesus clearly attributed His miraculous activity to the Holy Spirit (Matt. 12:28). The Holy Spirit was a prerequisite and absolute necessity in the life and ministry of Jesus. It was at His baptism in Jordan that the fullness of the Holy Spirit descended upon Him immediately prior to Him entering into the wilderness, and Him being *empowered for purpose.*

As our thoughts turn again to the events leading up to the closing chapters of our Lord's life, we consider the impact of the Holy Spirit upon His earthly ministry. As Easter approaches, we will spend the next forty days considering together how we can draw more deeply on the resources of the Holy Spirit as Jesus did during this significant experience of His life, propelling Him into His earthly ministry. Lent is that time of preparation by the Holy

Spirit for greater works of ministry in each of our lives.

Traditionally, Lent has three main elements. The first is a period of prayer and fasting, a self-emptying in order to receive more of the empowering of the Holy Spirit. Alongside that, the second is giving up something of significance, a period of abstinence, self-denial and self-restraint. The third is giving something out, by acts of self-sacrifice and deeds of kindness, by engaging in selfless acts of service, bringing support and help to some area of the community that we might not normally connect with. Jesus *gave up*, in order that He might *give out*.

Ash Wednesday, the name of the first day of Lent, comes from the practice of placing ashes mixed with oil on the foreheads of the faithful. The idea of oil and ash together is found in Isaiah 61:3: '... To give them beauty for ashes, The oil of joy for mourning ...' (NKJV). Oil is a physical symbol of the Holy Spirit, and ash a physical symbol of repentance; 'they would have repented ... in sackcloth and ashes' (Luke 10:13). Godly sorrow for sin, and repentance. At the outset of our study, invite the Holy Spirit to do a fresh and deeper work in your life, opening your heart in some moments of prayerful reflection and repentance.

*You will notice that in this book I have quoted from a number of different Bible translations besides the familiar NIV. When quoting particular verses of Scripture, I have chosen translations which I feel best depict the original language and sentiment. As a result, I hope you may find fresh insight into God's Word.*

# Passion ... Power ... Purpose ...
## *Endued from On High*

## Icebreaker

Take a handful of sweets of different colours, such as M&Ms. Each colour represents a part of life. For each sweet you hold, share something from the corresponding area of your life, then you may eat the sweets.

## Opening Prayer

Father, help me, I pray, over the next forty days, as I explore my thoughts and attitudes towards the Person, work and ministry of Your Holy Spirit. Help me to lay aside any preconceived thoughts and prejudices that may affect the full release and flow of Your Spirit's power in my life. Blessed Holy Spirit, help me to be open and willing to embrace all You are and all that You have to pour into my life. Lord, I commit in expectant anticipation my full participation and co-operation with You. I want to be filled afresh with Your Holy Spirit today so that I may be *empowered for purpose*. Come, Holy Spirit, come. Amen.

## Bible Readings

### Luke 3:21-22

When all the people were being baptised, Jesus was baptised too. And as he was praying, heaven was opened and the Holy Spirit descended on him in bodily form like a dove. And a voice came from heaven: 'You are my Son, whom I love; with you I am well pleased.'

### Luke 4:1-2

Jesus, full of the Holy Spirit, returned from the Jordan and was led by the Spirit in the desert, where for forty days he was tempted by the devil.

### Luke 4:14-19

Jesus returned to Galilee in the power of the Spirit, and news about him spread through the whole countryside. He taught in their synagogues, and everyone praised him.

He went to Nazareth, where he had been brought up, and on the Sabbath day he went into the synagogue, as was his custom. And he stood up to read. The scroll of the prophet Isaiah was handed to him. Unrolling it, he found the place where it is written:

'The Spirit of the Lord is on me,
  because he has anointed me
  to preach good news to the poor.
He has sent me to proclaim freedom for the prisoners
  and recovery of sight for the blind,
  to release the oppressed,
  to proclaim the year of the Lord's favour.'

## Eye Opener

The only offensive weapon listed in Paul's armoury in Ephesians 6 is the sword of the Spirit. Armour can protect, but only an effective offensive weapon will enable you to defeat and conquer your enemy. In the wilderness, Jesus takes hold of the eternal Word of truth. Armed with the Word which is 'quick, and powerful, and sharper than any two-edged sword' (Heb. 4:12, AV), He withstands the wiles of the devil, declaring boldly from the Old Testament, 'it is written ... it is written ... it is written ...' Full of the Holy Spirit, He defeated the devil with 'the sword of the Spirit, which is the word of God' (Eph. 6:17, AV).

## Setting the Scene

Luke's references to the Holy Spirit in connection with the life of Christ are very instructive. Jesus was born of the Virgin Mary through a direct intervention by the Holy Spirit. The angel answered Mary, 'The Holy Spirit will come upon you, and the power of the Most High

will overshadow you. So the holy one to be born will be called the Son of God' (Luke 1:35). Then, when Jesus was about thirty years of age, He received an entirely new experience of the Holy Spirit when He was baptised in the River Jordan.

In relation to His baptism, He said, '... it is proper for us to do this to fulfil all righteousness' (Matt. 3:15). His was a baptism of righteousness not repentance, a public proclamation of His right-standing with the Father. As He prayed, the heavens opened and the Holy Spirit descended upon Him visibly like a dove; '... John bore witness, saying, "I saw the Spirit descending from heaven like a dove, and He remained upon Him. I did not know Him, but He who sent me to baptize with water said to me, 'Upon whom you see the Spirit descending, and remaining on Him, this is He who baptizes with the Holy Spirit'"' (John 1:32–33, NKJV).

Jesus' Father declared, 'This is my Son, whom I love; with him I am well pleased' (Matt. 3:17). His right-standing was ratified in baptism, validated by the descent of the Holy Spirit and declared by the Father. The coming of the Holy Spirit upon Him at His baptism was an absolute necessity for the time of severe testing and temptation He would endure. 'Jesus, full of the Holy Spirit, returned from the Jordan ...' (Luke 4:1) and entered the wilderness. It was the fullness of the Holy Spirit that fortified and energised Him.

## Filled, Led, Empowered and Anointed

The work of the Holy Spirit in Christ's life during this time was the precursor to the commencement of His powerful ministry. Luke says that from His baptism in Jordan, being *'full* of the Holy Spirit' He was *'led* by the Spirit' into the wilderness (Luke 4:1, my emphasis). His entering the wilderness was also a work of the Spirit. Under the Spirit's leading, Jesus withdrew Himself from the world and remained detached from it for a time. It was a period when the Holy Spirit was working significantly in His life. The Holy Spirit was preparing, empowering and equipping Jesus for His years of public ministry. The Word of God sustained Him as He drew deeply on it, and the work of the Holy Spirit *empowered Him for purpose.*

Finally, when Jesus emerged from the desert experience, He returned to Galilee 'in the *power* of the Spirit' (Luke 4:14, my emphasis) to commence His public ministry. He went to the synagogue to announce His mission to the world in the words of the prophet Isaiah: 'The Spirit of the Lord is upon me because he has *anointed* me ...' (Luke 4:18, my emphasis). Then He immediately set about preaching the gospel of the kingdom of heaven and healing all that were oppressed by the devil (Mark 1:12–15).

Anointing is mentioned on a number of occasions in Scripture, both in the Old and New Testaments, usually in connection with anointing people with oil. Jesus referred to the practice of anointing with oil in relation to fasting (Matt. 6:17) and when He rebuked the disciples for not anointing His head with oil (Luke 7:46). Anointing with oil in Scripture signified the setting apart or consecration of a priest, prophet or king by God for a specific purpose, the Holy Spirit coming upon them to empower them to fulfil their purpose.

The forty days in the wilderness signifies a time of spiritual empowerment, spiritual preparation and spiritual anointing. It is important to be full of the Holy Spirit, but it is even more important to be empowered and anointed by Him for service and ministry. Jesus was anointed to 'preach good news to the poor ... to proclaim freedom for the prisoners ... recovery of sight for the blind, to release the oppressed, to proclaim the year of the Lord's favour' (Luke 4:18–19). This was the commission He passed to His disciples: 'As the Father has sent me, I am sending you'; 'Go into all the world and preach the good news ...' (John 20:21; Mark 16:15).

As the early disciples witnessed and experienced the powerful ministry of Jesus under the anointing of the Holy

Spirit, Jesus assured them that the same Holy Spirit who came upon Him at Jordan would come upon them: 'I am going to send you what my Father has promised; but stay in the city until you have been clothed with power from on high' (Luke 24:49). Jesus said to His disciples that because He was going to His Father they would do 'greater works' than those He performed (John 14:12, NKJV).

That is exactly what happened at Pentecost, the place of passion, power and purpose. The disciples waited in Jerusalem for the fulfilment. As the Holy Spirit descended upon them, they no longer hid away 'because they were afraid' (Mark 16:8) but were emboldened, energised and *empowered for purpose* – the purpose of fulfilling the great commission Jesus had put in their charge. The fearful and timid group became unrecognisable as they were transformed by the power of the Holy Spirit for service. They immediately went out to the people of the city declaring Christ crucified, the forgiveness of sins through salvation and the power of a resurrection life. Like Jesus, they were now *empowered for purpose*. God is eager to dwell in our lives through His Holy Spirit, and will do everything in His power to enable us to live the Spirit-empowered life, if we are willing to receive His fullness.

## Discussion Starters

1. What do you think repentance is really about?

_____

_____

_____

_____

_____

2. Look at Luke 3:8. What might be some fruits of repentance?

_____

_____

_____

_____

_____

3. In your opinion, how significant is water baptism?

_____

_____

_____

_____

_____

4. What are you willing to give up for Lent? What act of selfless service will you engage in during Lent?

_____

_____

_____

_____

5. What do you think it means to be 'full' of the Holy Spirit?

_____

_____

_____

_____

_____

6. How does spiritual anointing relate to practical engagement?

_____

_____

_____

_____

_____

7. What is the main reason that the Spirit was given? What are the other reasons?

_____

_____

_____

_____

_____

## Closing Prayer

Lord, I open my heart and life to a fresh flow of the Spirit. I know You are willing to give as much of the Holy Spirit to me as I am willing to receive, and I open myself up to receive more and more of Him. Come, Holy Spirit, fill me anew. Amen.

## Final Thoughts

John the Baptist declared, 'I baptise you with water ...
He will baptise you with the Holy Spirit and with fire'
(Matt. 3:11). When John uttered these words, he was
announcing and ushering in the age of the Holy Spirit. John
baptised with water but pointed to the One who was coming
who would baptise with the Holy Spirit and with fire.

Jesus promised His disciples that when He returned to
His Father, He would send from on high the gift of the
Holy Spirit to empower them, and as a result they would
be effective witnesses for Him; 'But you will receive
power when the Holy Spirit comes on you; and you will
be my witnesses ...' (Acts 1:8).

The promised fire fell at Pentecost, transforming them
from fearful, hesitant disciples into men and women of
holy boldness. It truly was a baptism of fire that turned
them into blazing incendiaries who turned the then
known world upside down (Acts 17:6, AV). To be filled
with the Spirit emboldens and empowers us to testify
freely and witness openly to the saving grace of our God
in Jesus, turning us from the fearful into the fearless; as
the writer of the Proverbs says, making 'the righteous ...
as bold as a lion' (Prov. 28:1).

## Further Study

Matthew 3; Joel 2:28; John 16:13; 20:22; Romans 8:14;
2 Corinthians 1:21; Ephesians 6:10–18; Hebrews 1:9; 4:12;
2 Timothy 3:16; 2 Peter 1:21; Acts 2; 4:8–14,23–33; 6:3–10;
7:51–56; 8:17; 10:34–48; 11:24; 14:1–17; 16:6–10; 19:8;
21:37–40.

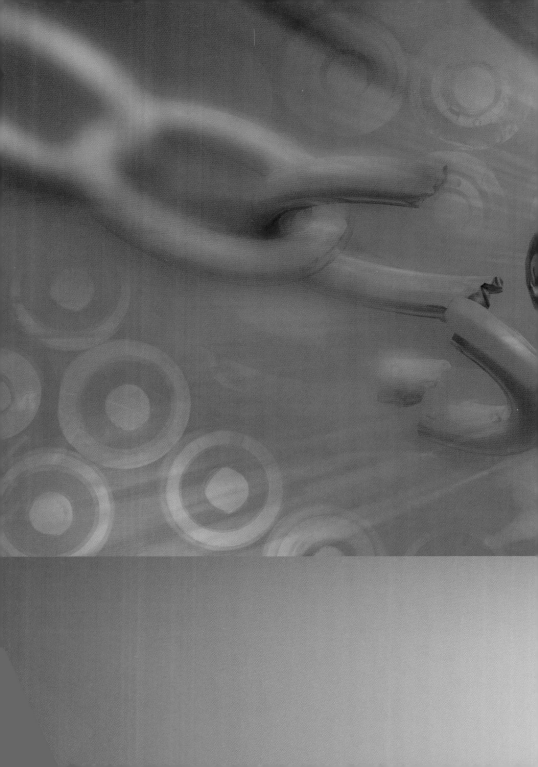

# Released in the Spirit ...
*Energised for Life*

## Icebreaker

When you think of the word 'energy', what picture immediately comes to your mind and why? Share with other members of the group what energises you.

## Opening Prayer

Lord, I am grateful that the promise You gave to Your disciples also includes me today. Descend upon my heart, taking away indifference and coldness. Touch my heart and lips with the same fire that fell on those early disciples, so that my life and witness is utterly transformed and energised. I want to experience all that Your Holy Spirit can do in me and through me. Teach me how to open myself up more fully to a deeper work of Your Holy Spirit, and let the divine invasion and indwelling of His power be my daily experience. Amen.

## Bible Readings

### Zechariah 4:6

So he said to me ... 'Not by might nor by power, but by my Spirit,' says the LORD Almighty.

### Joel 2:28-29

... I will pour out my Spirit on all people. Your sons and daughters will prophesy, your old men will dream dreams, your young men will see visions. Even on my servants, both men and women, I will pour out my Spirit in those days.

### Luke 24:49

I am going to send you what my Father has promised; but stay in the city until you have been clothed with power from on high.

### Acts 2:38

Peter replied, 'Repent and be baptised, every one of you, in the name of Jesus Christ for the forgiveness of your sins. And you will receive the gift of the Holy Spirit.'

**Acts 8:14-17**

When the apostles in Jerusalem heard that Samaria had accepted the word of God, they sent Peter and John to them. When they arrived, they prayed for them that they might receive the Holy Spirit, because the Holy Spirit had not yet come upon any of them; they had simply been baptised into the name of the Lord Jesus. Then Peter and John placed their hands on them, and they received the Holy Spirit.

## Eye Opener

The distinctive expression and ministry of the Holy Spirit is to give life. The second verse of the Bible says, '... the earth was formless and empty, darkness covered the surface of the watery depths, and the Spirit of God was hovering over the surface of the waters' (Gen. 1:2, HCSB). The Holy Spirit played a major role in the creation of the universe, and He was also the agency for producing life and energy in man. How do we know this? Job 33:4 (AV) says, 'The Spirit of God hath made me, and the breath of the Almighty hath given me life'.

## Setting the Scene

As well as being the genesis of life (Gen. 1:2), the Spirit of God also brings new life. Jesus said, '... unless one is born of water and the Spirit, he cannot enter the kingdom of God' (John 3:5, NKJV). We are regenerated by the indwelling work of God's Spirit: 'For the law of the Spirit of life in Christ Jesus has made me free from the law of sin and death' (Rom. 8:2, NKJV). There is also a further dimension to life in the Spirit. The Holy Spirit imparts to us the empowered, energised life if we are willing to receive it. As we have seen, this happened in the life of

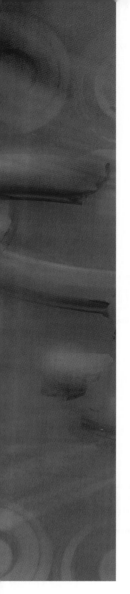

Jesus, at Jordan and in the wilderness. It also happened at Pentecost, where the waiting disciples were endued from on high as the Holy Spirit descended on them. If we are to fulfil the Great Commission of Jesus, like Jesus and the disciples we need to expose ourselves afresh to this energising dimension of the Holy Spirit's ministry. God wants to clothe His people with a supply of the Spirit's power that will enable us to be *empowered for purpose* and to experience the same degree of impact in this generation as the Early Church did in theirs, if not more.

God wants us, His people, to demonstrate to the world that the supernatural signs, wonders and miracles of the Gospels and Early Church are also a part of His purposes today: 'Go into all the world and preach the good news to all creation ... And these signs will accompany those who believe ...' (Mark 16:15–18). God's programme for His Church today is to preach the Word with signs following.

Although the ministry of the Holy Spirit in the Old Testament was intermittent, Joel prophesied that a day would come when He would be permanently poured out on all flesh.

## The Promised Holy Spirit

Jesus declared, '"Whoever believes in me, as the Scripture has said, streams of living water will flow from within him." By this he meant the Spirit, whom those who believed in him were later to receive' (John 7:38–39). He said, 'If you then, though you are evil, know how to give good gifts to your children, how much more will your Father in heaven give the Holy Spirit to those who ask him!' (Luke 11:13).

Different views are held about the infilling of the Spirit. Some say it takes place at conversion, others say it is a separate and ensuing experience, accompanied by speaking in tongues or other manifestations and expressions. John Wesley talked about receiving 'the second blessing'. There is no question that when the promised Holy Spirit fell at Pentecost, significant things happened and extraordinary expressions and manifestations were witnessed, so much so that onlookers said, 'They have had too much wine' (Acts 2:13). Whatever our view of the doctrine of the Holy Spirit or whatever experience we may have had of Him in the past, we need to be full of the Holy Spirit today. If we do not enjoy a continuous and ever-present spiritually energising flow of His power and presence, we are not living according to the New Testament pattern.

Ephesians 5:18 gives the command 'be filled with the Spirit'. This was not an optional extra for consideration, but an absolute requirement. The verb 'be filled' in Greek is the present continuous tense, better translated 'be being filled'. This is not a once only, one-off spiritual experience during or subsequent to conversion, but the ongoing release of the Spirit's work, energising, equipping, enabling and empowering our lives. And this is a command because so many things demand our attention, forcing their way into our lives, making the Spirit's work marginal and peripheral, rather than central.

'Don't get your stimulus from wine (for there is always the danger of excessive drinking), but let the Spirit stimulate your souls' (Eph. 5:18, Phillips). A drunk man loses all track of time, is totally disorganised, out of control, slothful, ill-disciplined and irresponsible. Getting drunk debilitates and disorientates. Paul says the Spirit-filled life is not like this. Instead it is disciplined, vital, vibrant and dynamic. As we have noted, observers on the Day of Pentecost suggested the disciples were drunk. They were so astonished and could find no other explanation, but Peter got up and lucidly, with great oratory, delivered a masterpiece of a sermon on the resurrection. That's what being filled with the Spirit can do. Paul doesn't say, 'Manage your time better', but 'Make the best use of your time' (Eph. 5:16, Phillips) by being filled with the Spirit. The Holy Spirit energises, invigorates, directs and empowers us to lead abundant, productive,

orderly, stress-free lives, *empowered for purpose*.

Jesus said to His followers, '… you will receive power when the Holy Spirit has come upon you …' (Acts 1:8, NASB). 'Power' here is the Greek word *dunamis*, from which we derive the word 'dynamo'. A dynamo, or turbine, provides a continual source of energy and power, giving momentum, movement and drive that builds and builds and never stops flowing. If the production of natural, mechanical energy can make such an impact in our daily lives, how much more so the supernatural energy delivered by the Holy Spirit.

The Holy Spirit imparts and wraps the mantle of His divine presence and power around our shoulders to enable us to undertake great exploits in Christ's name. We saw in the previous study that this was the mantle of power upon Jesus which He received at His baptism, the anointing which continually rested upon Him while He was ministering here on earth. That is what He has now made available to us through His death, resurrection and ascension, sending the Holy Spirit on the Day of Pentecost. It is the divine presence of the Spirit that enables us to receive the anointing of supernatural energising. If you have not received the releasing, energising work of the Holy Spirit, be assured that such an experience awaits you.

## Discussion Starters

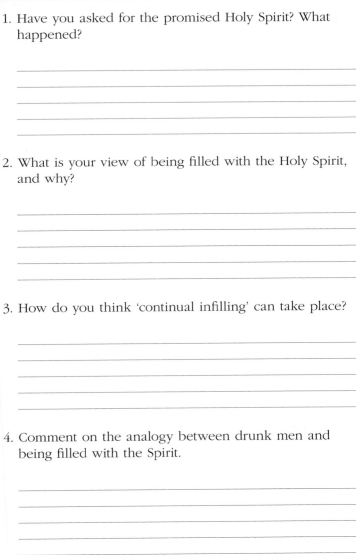

1. Have you asked for the promised Holy Spirit? What happened?

2. What is your view of being filled with the Holy Spirit, and why?

3. How do you think 'continual infilling' can take place?

4. Comment on the analogy between drunk men and being filled with the Spirit.

5. How do you feel about receiving 'the mantle'?

_____

_____

_____

_____

_____

6. What are some of the recorded happenings in our readings for this study?

_____

_____

_____

_____

_____

7. Do you feel the need for a fresh infilling of the Holy Spirit?

_____

_____

_____

_____

_____

## Closing Prayer

Lord, in the words of the hymn writer I pray, 'Spirit of the living God,/Fall afresh on me ... Break me, melt me, mould me, fill me./Spirit of the living God,/Fall afresh on me.'[1] Lord, I ask that this will be my experience, even this day. Amen.

## Final Thought

Paul tells us that we are sealed with the Holy Spirit
(Eph. 4:30) as a mark of God's ownership. More than that,
'the promised Holy Spirit ... is a deposit guaranteeing
our inheritance until the redemption of those who are
God's possession' (Eph. 1:13–14). He is the deposit or
down payment – there is more to come. The Holy Spirit
is God's pledge and guarantee of the full provision of
His energising power and presence, made available in
Christ. He is appointed executor of the divine will here
on earth, making available the abundant power of God.
It is possible to have an inheritance, yet never enter into
the good of it. Maybe because we don't know about it
or because, although we do know, we just aren't able to
believe it is possible to claim. The Holy Spirit is given to
us to guarantee and make available the energising mantle
of God's power in our lives. Remember, you must put
the plug into the socket before receiving electricity. Let's
determine to be like Elisha, who setting himself to receive
Elijah's mantle of power from on high, did not let him
out of his sight until he received it, and then went on to
perform twice as many miracles as his predecessor.

## Further Study

2 Kings 2:1–18; Mark 16:15–20; Luke 2:25; John 1:32; 7:39;
Acts 7:55; 13:9; 19:1–20; Romans 8:11; 15:18–20;
1 Corinthians 2:4; Ephesians 5:15–20; 1 Thessalonians 1:5;
2 Timothy 1:7; 3:5; 1 Peter 4:14; 1 John 4:13.

Note
    1. 'Spirit of the Living God', Daniel Iverson (1977), copyright © 1935
Birdwing Music/EMI CMP BV Holland/Small Stone Media (Admin. By
Song Solutions Daybreak, 14 Horsted Square, Uckfield, East Sussex TN22
1QG, info@songsolutions.org). Used by permission.

# Growing in the Spirit ...
## *Enriched in Character*

## Icebreaker

Put a bowl of nine different fruits in the centre of the room. Each member of the group is to choose the fruit he or she likes best and explain why.

## Opening Prayer

Blessed Holy Spirit, I am thankful that You are working in me to produce the image of the Lord Jesus Christ. May His nature and character shine through me more and more every day. Holy Spirit of purity and power, rest upon me, give me in equal measure both purity and power. Help me to be fruitful with Christlike qualities enriching my life and relationships. Father, I want to keep all my channels open so that the fruit of the Spirit may grow and grow in abundance. I ask this for the praise and honour of Your wonderful name. Amen.

## Bible Readings

### Galatians 5:16–23

So I say, live by the Spirit, and you will not gratify the desires of the sinful nature. For the sinful nature desires what is contrary to the Spirit, and the Spirit what is contrary to the sinful nature. They are in conflict with each other, so that you do not do what you want. But if you are led by the Spirit, you are not under law. The acts of the sinful nature are obvious: sexual immorality, impurity and debauchery; idolatry and witchcraft; hatred, discord, jealousy, fits of rage, selfish ambition, dissensions, factions and envy; drunkenness, orgies, and the like … But the fruit of the Spirit is love, joy, peace, patience, kindness, goodness, faithfulness, gentleness and self-control. Against such things there is no law.

### 1 Corinthians 13:4–7,13

Love is patient, love is kind. It does not envy, it does

not boast, it is not proud. It is not rude, it is not self-seeking, it is not easily angered, it keeps no record of wrongs. Love does not delight in evil but rejoices with the truth. It always protects, always trusts, always hopes, always perseveres ... And now these three remain: faith, hope and love. But the greatest of these is love.

## Eye Opener

In the last session we looked at the energising power of the Holy Spirit, but this session we look at the enriching qualities He bestows. God only entrusts divine resources to those who have the character to handle them well. God will not entrust His gifts to those with character flaws. Here I am not talking about the ongoing work of the Spirit in us, but the entrusting of power into the hands of those who are not yet ready for it (see Acts 8:14–24). Part of the Holy Spirit's ministry is to prepare us to handle His power and gifts, and He does this by enriching our lives with His graces. We must always remember that the Bible describes Him as the *Holy* Spirit, underlining His character of holiness, righteousness and purity, as well as His power and purpose.

## Setting the Scene

Today in the Church there are those who focus primarily on the demonstration of the Spirit's power, the gifts, miracles, manifestations, signs and wonders. On the other hand, there are some who shy away from these things and put their focus on the sanctifying work of the Spirit, emphasising the doctrine of holiness, purity and separation. But both of these aspects are part of the Spirit's work in our lives. Holiness, purity and obedience are important dimensions of the Holy Spirit's *empowering for purpose*. We are to be set apart *from* sin, 'through sanctification of the Spirit, unto obedience' (1 Pet. 1:2, AV)

and we are to be set apart *to* act in His purpose and His power; 'my message ... [was] not with wise and persuasive words, but with a demonstration of the Spirit's power' (1 Cor. 2:4). It is the Holy Spirit who forms the character of Christ within us. His work produces our development and growth into Christlikeness, transforming us to be more and more like our Saviour. The theme of these studies is *empowered for purpose*. Have you ever considered God's primary purpose for your life? We saw at the Jordan that God was so pleased with His Son that He wants you and me to become just like Him: 'This is My beloved Son, in whom I am well pleased' (Matt. 17:5, NKJV); '... God decided that those who came to him ... should become like His Son ...' (Rom. 8:29, TLB). The Holy Spirit has been sent not only to empower us from without with His anointing, to achieve that great purpose, but also to enrich us from within, with the qualities of Christ's nature and the characteristics of the Christ life, the fruit of the Spirit.

## Growing in the Graces

Well, what is the fruit of the Spirit? It is the Spirit's work of supernatural enriching in our lives. Just a short glance at the fruit of the Spirit in Galatians 5, and we see portrayed the personality characteristics of the Lord Jesus: 'love, joy, peace, patience, kindness, goodness, faithfulness, gentleness and self-control' (vv.22–23). The fruit of the Spirit is personified in Jesus.

This passage is often referred to as the 'fruits' of the Spirit, but the word is actually singular, one fruit with different qualities or flavours. Think of your favourite fruits, and imagine their distinctive flavours combined in one perfect fruit. The first fruit of the Spirit is *love* (v.22). The characteristics that follow are love in motion. Love is not a feeling but a person. 'God is love' (1 John 4:8), and Jesus is the embodiment of that love: '... God was in Christ ...' (2 Cor. 5:19, NKJV). When the Spirit produces the fruit of love in us, we develop the capacity to love like Jesus.

Have you ever seen someone who has just fallen in love, and witnessed the natural outflow of joy and excitement that instinctively follows? *Joy* is the outcome of that love. Isaiah puts it like this: 'Therefore with joy shall ye draw water out of the wells of salvation' (Isa. 12:3, AV). Having received God's love, we experience a joy that defies comprehension. That joy gives way to deep settled *peace* and contentment. Peace is joy at rest. No struggle, no stress, no strain, '... righteousness, peace and joy in the Holy Spirit ...' (Rom. 14:17). Paul said, '... for I have learned, in whatsoever state I am, therewith to be content' (Phil. 4:11, AV).

The outworking of that peace is *patience* and longsuffering; '... bearing fruit in every good work ... strengthened with all power, according to the might of his glory, unto all patience and longsuffering with joy ...' (Col. 1:10–11, ASV). Wow! We live in an impatient, demanding society that wants everything now or yesterday. We are victims of the 'microwave mentality'. But patience is the evidence of love, love is patient, love suffers long (1 Cor. 13:3–4). It is not demanding, whining, impatient or intolerant, but considerate and understanding; '... walk worthy ... with longsuffering, forbearing one another in love ...' (Eph. 4:1–2, AV). Patience produces *kindness*; 'We are patient and kind. We serve him in the power of the Holy Spirit. We serve him with true love' (2 Cor. 6:6, NIRV) and kindness is the expression of *goodness*.

I came across a great definition of love in a book by the American evangelist of yesteryear, Charles Finney. He said, 'Love is bringing about the highest possible good in another individual's life'. This is the intrinsic goodness of love that wants the best for everyone; '... God anointed Jesus of Nazareth with the Holy Spirit and with power, who went about doing good and healing all ...' (Acts 10:38, NKJV). At the heart of God's love is His *faithfulness*, His covenant commitment, His unequivocal eternal promises:

'Every good and perfect gift is from above, coming down from the Father ... who does not change like shifting shadows' (James 1:17). Goodness and kindness are not harsh or brutal, but display *gentleness* and sensitivity, as did the Holy Spirit when He descended on Jesus in the form of a hovering dove. Jesus said we are to be as harmless, innocent and gentle as doves (Matt. 10:16). Paul finishes his descriptive characteristics, of the fruit of love with *self-control*. This is not simply achieved through determined doggedness or self-effort, but is the control of love: 'For the love of Christ controls us ...' (2 Cor. 5:14, NASB). When we love fully, all aspects of the fruit of the Spirit enrich our lives. This truly is the Spirit controlled life, the real substance of our Christian faith (Col. 1:8). Truly the fruit of the Spirit enriches us, to be *empowered for purpose*, to love as we have been loved.

## Discussion Starters

1. Discuss the idea that Paul said 'fruit' of the Spirit not 'fruits' of the Spirit.

_____

_____

_____

_____

_____

2. Discuss Charles Finney's definition of love.

_____

_____

_____

_____

_____

3. Consider the account of the Samaritan in Luke 10:29–37, and the aspects of the fruit of the Spirit displayed.

_____

_____

_____

_____

_____

4. In what practical ways does the fruit of the Spirit evidence itself in our lives?

_____

_____

_____

_____

_____

5. What might be some of the reasons why our own sense of peace gets disturbed?

_____

_____

_____

_____

_____

6. Think of some Bible characters who showed great patience.

_____

_____

_____

_____

_____

7. What are the differences between being longsuffering and being indifferent?

_____

_____

_____

_____

_____

### Closing Prayer

Father, we echo the words of the old hymn writer: 'Spirit divine, O quicken us now,/Whilst in your presence, humbly we bow,/Set all our hearts ablaze with your love,/Teach us the secret of life from above'.[1] Amen.

## Final Thought

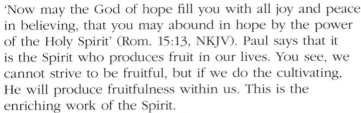

'Now may the God of hope fill you with all joy and peace in believing, that you may abound in hope by the power of the Holy Spirit' (Rom. 15:13, NKJV). Paul says that it is the Spirit who produces fruit in our lives. You see, we cannot strive to be fruitful, but if we do the cultivating, He will produce fruitfulness within us. This is the enriching work of the Spirit.

Galatians 5 contrasts the works of the flesh (vv.16–21) with the fruit of the Spirit; the self-focused self-effort, produced by our own energy and striving, with the deep work and outgrowth of the Sprit's enriching. When we are filled with the Spirit, walking in His ways, and allowing the soil of our lives to be enriched, the fruit of the Spirit is the natural outworking of growth. It is the work of the indwelling Spirit that enriches us to live in godly ways, displaying the character and nature of Christ. These nine qualities of life are the outworking of the Spirit abiding within. Paul is quite emphatic in his assertion: 'Walk in the Spirit, and you shall not fulfill the lust of the flesh' (Gal. 5:16, NKJV).

## Further Study

Romans 5:1–5; 8:6; 12:12; 14:17; 1 Corinthians 9:27; 2 Corinthians 5:14; 6:6; Ephesians 3:14–19; 4:32; Philippians 4:7; Colossians 1:1–14; 3:12–17; 1 Thessalonians 1:6; 2 Timothy 1:7; James 3:13–18; 2 Peter 1:1–8.

Note

1. E.C.W. Boulton, 'Floods of revival, Lord let them fall' © Joyce Woodstock. Used by permission.

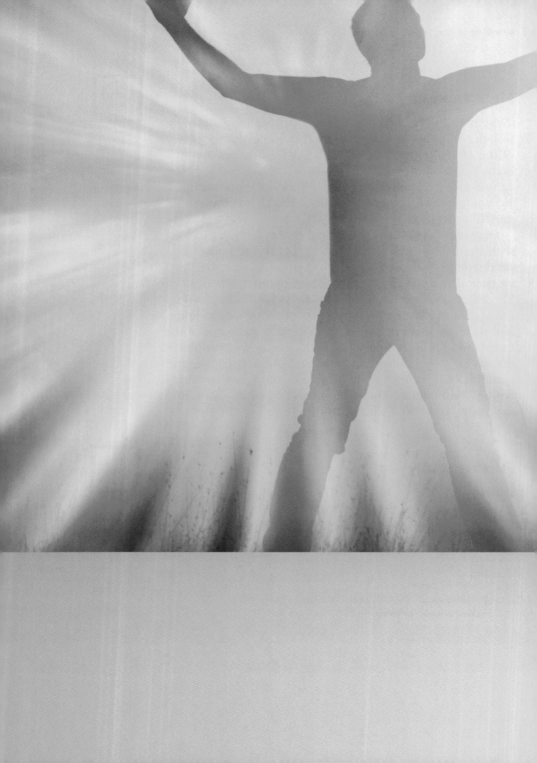

# The Third Dimension ...
## *Enlightened Within*

## Icebreaker

If there was one thing you were given the power to be able to do, to bring about a change in this world or a change in you, what would it be and why?

## Opening Prayer

Father, I recognise the strong pull of this world, and the tendency of my own heart to be distracted and drawn away from You. During this study, bring a fresh spiritual awareness to me, I pray, and cause my spirit to be open and alert as never before. Lord, I am growing tired of the inner struggles that so often threaten to tear me apart. Come by Your Holy Spirit, connect afresh with my spirit in such a way that I will be *empowered for purpose*, freed from those things that would hold me back. Amen.

## Bible Readings

### 1 Thessalonians 5:23-24

May God himself, the God of peace, sanctify you through and through. May your whole spirit, soul and body be kept blameless at the coming of our Lord Jesus Christ. The one who calls you is faithful and he will do it.

### Ephesians 3:16 (HCSB)

I pray that He may grant you, according to the riches of His glory, to be strengthened with power through His Spirit in the inner man.

### Hebrews 4:12-13

For the word of God is living and active. Sharper than any double-edged sword, it penetrates even to dividing soul and spirit, joints and marrow; it judges the thoughts and attitudes of the heart. Nothing in all creation is hidden from God's sight.

### Luke 1:46-47

And Mary said: 'My soul glorifies the Lord and my

spirit rejoices in God my Saviour ...'

**John 13:21**

After he had said this, Jesus was troubled in spirit ...

**Luke 23:46**

Jesus called out with a loud voice, 'Father, into your hands I commit my spirit.'

**Romans 8:2,16**

... through Christ Jesus the law of the Spirit of life set me free from the law of sin and death ... The Spirit himself testifies with our spirit that we are God's children.

## Eye Opener

Last session, we considered the enriching work of the Spirit, recognising it is His work in us producing fruitfulness; the Spirit-controlled temperament. But, there is a problem – the flesh! 'For the flesh sets its desire against the Spirit ... for these are in opposition to one another ...' (Gal. 5:17, NASB). Paul identifies a struggle, the flesh tugging in the opposite direction, seeking to draw us into all ungodliness. So what is the flesh? Well, it refers to the basic instincts and desires of the human nature corrupted by sin, however, we can 'Walk in the Spirit, and ... not fulfill the lust of the flesh' (Gal. 5:16, NKJV).

## Setting the Scene

'After beginning with the Spirit, are you now trying to attain your goal by human effort?' (Gal. 3:3). The deeds of the flesh come easily to us. Somehow we don't need to be taught them; we effortlessly slip back into them. They seem to come quite naturally to us as part of the legacy Adam bequeathed us. One of the works of the Holy Spirit is to bring the awareness of their pull, by conviction of righteousness and sin to our lives (John 16:8). If the Spirit is at work in our lives, and the deeds of the flesh seek to assert themselves, the warning bell of God's conviction

sounds in our spirits. As we respond to Him, our spirits are touched and we are empowered to walk in the ways of the Spirit.

Tennyson wrote the words, 'And ah for a man to rise in me,/That the man I am may cease to be'.[1] That is the cry of many hearts, struggling to overcome the corruption of the human soul. The fleshly man controlled by the instincts of the soul, suppresses his spirit. Paul needed to write to the church at Corinth, 'I … could not speak unto you as unto spiritual, but as unto carnal …' (1 Cor. 3:1, AV). The work of the Spirit enables us not to fulfil the desires of the flesh, bringing strength to the spirit man: '… being strengthened with all power according to his glorious might so that you may have great endurance and patience, and joyfully giving thanks to the Father …' (Col. 1:11–12). We need to open up our own spirit within – 'the spirit man' – and yield to a deeper and fresh work of His Spirit, so that our spirit is fully alive to the Holy Spirit.

## The Spirit(ual) Man

'May God himself, the God of peace, sanctify you through and through. May your whole spirit, soul and body be kept blameless at the coming of our Lord Jesus Christ' (1 Thess. 5:23). This is a key verse in understanding the design of God in the human personality. We all have three distinct yet integrated parts to our being; it's the way God made us, a trinity of parts comprised of spirit, soul and body. We are not three people in one, but Scripture does identify three distinct parts to our being. Some believe that the spirit and soul are one and the same thing, but in the verse above, two distinct and separate Greek words are used for 'spirit' and 'soul', *psuche* and *pneuma*. There is no doubt that the human spirit is distinctive. We have a body, a soul and a *spirit*, 'the spirit(ual) man'. When a Christian is out of touch with the Lord in his spirit, it isn't long before his soul is affected, and what affects the soul, affects the body also.

When we come to know Christ, the human spirit, dead towards God, becomes alive to the transforming power of Jesus. Paul describes this human spirit as the 'inner man' which God wants to '... strengthen ... with power through his Spirit ...' (Eph. 3:16). The Holy Spirit wants to engage His power to the very real spiritual struggles we face. He longs to connect with the spirit(ual) man at the core of his being. First enlightening our spirits, in turn impacting our soul and body, which is sanctified by the Holy Spirit (1 Pet. 1:2) becoming '... a temple of the Holy Spirit ...' (1 Cor. 6:19).

We cannot eliminate our natural drives or urges, although sometimes we try in vain to suppress or repress them. Paul identifies them as the old, or carnal, nature. But when we receive the new nature in Christ, he says that we can 'be renewed in the spirit of [our] mind[s]' (Eph 4:23, AV). If we allow the power of the Holy Spirit in all of His fullness to elevate the spirit(ual) man, then 'if by the Spirit you put to death the misdeeds of the body, you will live ...' (Rom. 8:13). We will be able to live in the liberty and good of the Spirit-controlled life, according to the divine order in which God created us to function. We will never be free from the presence and impact of sin, but we can be free from its power and control (2 Cor. 3:17).

Paul, reflecting on his own struggles in Romans chapter 7, makes this wonderful declaration: 'Therefore, there is now no condemnation for those who are in Christ Jesus, because through Christ Jesus the law of the Spirit of life set me free from the law of sin and death' (Rom. 8:1–2). Then he goes on in chapter 8 to describe graphically the power, liberty and freedom that comes from the Spirit.

The strengthening and growing of the spirit(ual) man, is dependent on our awareness and sensitivity to the Holy Spirit's conviction. As we have seen, He is holy, and because He is holy, He searches, confronts and convicts of sin. He enlightens us as we bring our sin to the cross; contrition and forgiveness pave the way to His presence

and power. The spirit(ual) man is where the Holy Spirit connects in our innermost beings, and does His deepest empowering work. On the last day of the feast, Jesus said He wanted to give to us the Holy Spirit in such a way that out of our 'innermost being [would] flow rivers of living water. But this He spoke of the Spirit ...' (John 7:38–39, NASB). Learn to walk in surrender to Him, and whenever you feel those carnal desires, call on Him to enlighten you afresh, 'that the eyes of your heart may be enlightened in order that you may know the hope to which he has called you' (Eph. 1:18).

## Discussion Starters

1. What are the characteristics of spirit, soul and body?

_____

_____

_____

_____

_____

2. Think of some ways in which the parts of our being interact.

_____

_____

_____

_____

_____

3. Taking Galatians 5:16–21, identify some ways in which we easily slip into the ways of the flesh.

_____

_____

_____

_____

_____

4. Look up as many Bible references as you can find on the conscience.

_____

_____

_____

_____

_____

5. Think through the idea of the spirit(ual) man being convinced of righteousness as being different from being convicted of sin.

_____

_____

_____

_____

_____

6. Explore the idea in Ephesians 4:22–32 of how can we 'put off' the natural man and then 'put on' the spiritual man.

_____

_____

_____

_____

_____

## Closing Prayer

O Lord, I bring to You the struggle I so often feel within me, and surrender myself afresh for cleansing and correction. I tune my spirit to You; strengthen me with power through Your Spirit in my inner man. I ask this in Jesus' name. Amen.

## Final Thought

'I say then: Walk in the Spirit and you shall not fulfill the lust of the flesh' (Gal. 5:16, NKJV). 'Walk' here in the Greek, means 'to keep in step'. Keeping in step with the Spirit is recognising and admitting when we are out of step, and getting back in step with Him. The Holy Spirit responds to obedience. Peter said, '… the Holy Spirit whom God has given to those who obey Him' (Acts 5:32, NKJV).

'Do not stifle the Holy Spirit' (1 Thess. 5:19, NLT). That means, do not close your spirit by allowing the works of the flesh to shut out the Holy Spirit, preventing His deeper work. Rather, be open in your spirit so that 'God's Spirit touches our spirits and confirms who we really are. We know who he is, and we know who we are ...' (Rom. 8:16–17, *The Message*). As we come to the end of this study, we must ask ourselves, are we giving in to the desires of the flesh or are we enlightened in the Spirit? Let the spirit(ual) man arise, energised by His Spirit, and let us be strong in Spirit, mighty in character and powerful in influence. *Empowered for purpose.*

## Further Study

Genesis 2:1–7; Proverbs 18:14; Matthew 26:41; Luke 1:80; 2:40; John 3:3–8; 4:23–24; 6:63; 7:35–41; 16:8–11; Romans 7–8; 15:16; 1 Corinthians 2:1–12; 6:18–20; 2 Corinthians 3:6,17; Galatians 5:1–18, 6:8; Ephesians 3:14–20; 4:20–32; Philippians 3:3; 2 Timothy 4:22; Philemon 25.

---

Note
  1. Alfred, Lord Tennyson (1809–1892), *Maud* Part 1, Verse X.

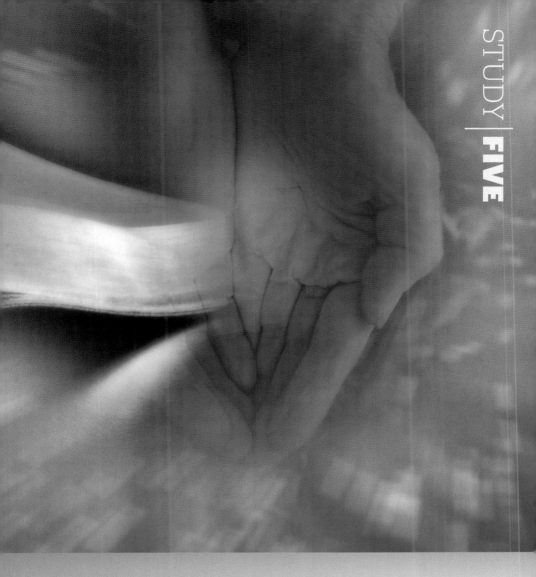

# The Giver of Gifts ...
*Equipped to Serve*

## Icebreaker

From a bowl of small gifts, each take a gift and express what you think about it and how you might use it. What other gift might you have preferred?

## Opening Prayer

Father, I realise how ineffective is Your Church without the Spirit. Give me, I pray, an understanding of the gifts of the Spirit and their importance, and a fresh desire to seek and express them in harmony with the Spirit's control. Lord, help me to gain a greater understanding of the supernatural nature of Your Church. I am grateful I do not have to rely only upon natural talent and human endeavour, that I can offer them to You. Take me, I pray, from my natural abilities into Your supernatural enabling. Help me to discover and embrace those gifts You would have me seek from You. Amen.

## Bible Readings

### 1 Corinthians 12:8-11

To one there is given through the Spirit the message of wisdom, to another the message of knowledge by means of the same Spirit, to another faith by the same Spirit, to another gifts of healing by that one Spirit, to another miraculous powers, to another prophecy, to another distinguishing between spirits, to another speaking in different kinds of tongues, and to still another the interpretation of tongues. All these are the work of one and the same Spirit, and he gives them to each one, just as he determines.

### 1 Corinthians 12:28-31

And in the church God has appointed first of all apostles, second prophets, third teachers, then workers of miracles, also those having gifts of healing, those able to help others, those with gifts of administration, and those speaking in different kinds of tongues.

**1 Corinthians 13:1–2**

If I speak in the tongues of men and of angels, but have not love, I am only a resounding gong or a clanging cymbal. If I have the gift of prophecy and can fathom all mysteries and all knowledge, and if I have a faith that can move mountains, but have not love, I am nothing.

## Eye Opener

The subject of spiritual gifts is found in a number of New Testament passages, but in relation to the gifts of the Spirit, particularly in 1 Corinthians chapters 12–14. The predominant theme in each chapter is distinct. In the twelfth chapter, the necessity of the spiritual gifts is set out, and the Church's need of them. The familiar 'love chapter', chapter 13, follows on, outlining and underlining the motivational power of love that must underpin our operation and functioning. The fourteenth chapter then gives clear instruction concerning the operation of the gifts, their purpose, and to what end and use the gifts are given.

## Setting the Scene

The enabling gifts of the Holy Spirit identified in 1 Corinthians 12 are supernatural gifts. In verses 8–11, Paul uses a number of distinctive words to present the nine gifts of the Spirit. In verse 1, he starts off, 'Now about spiritual gifts, brothers ...' In the Greek, only one word is used here for 'spiritual gifts' – *pneumatikoito*, which is probably more accurately translated 'supernaturals' or 'spirituals'. This word is derived from *pneuma*, another Greek word used in Scripture to describe the Holy Spirit of God. The word carries the idea of a supernatural intervention, actuated by the Holy Spirit, which transcends our natural ability and human

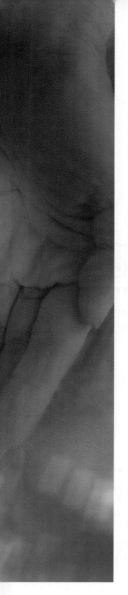

comprehension. From *pneumatikoito* in the first verse, the apostle moves on in the fourth verse to say, 'there are different kinds of gifts'. The word 'gifts' here is the word *charismata*, describing the diversities of the Holy Spirit's supernatural gifts. *Charismata* is the plural of the Greek word *charisma*, meaning 'gift', which in turn is derived from the word *charis* meaning 'grace'. Paul often used it in his writings. The result of God's grace is the impartation of the gift of the Holy Spirit. The Holy Spirit comes to us with His gifts, *charismata*. These nine gifts, then, are given and administered by the Holy Spirit for supernatural purposes. If we eliminate the miraculous element from our faith, we remove and deny the supernatural work of the Holy Spirit. That's why Paul says in verse 4 that all these gifts are inspired by 'the same Spirit'. Paul goes on not only to underline the necessity of receiving these gifts, but also gives instruction in the exercising of them, for the wellbeing and blessing of the Body of Christ, and the extension of God's kingdom in the world.

## The Gifts of the Spirit

So let's look at the diversity of the gifts. Paul says that we should not remain ignorant about them. 'Now concerning spiritual gifts, brethren, I would not have you ignorant' (1 Cor. 12:1, AV). That means we need to have a clear understanding of what makes them distinctive, and their supernatural character. They are bestowed upon believers, not for their personal benefit, but 'for the strengthening of the church' (1 Cor. 14:26).

*A word of knowledge* and *a word of wisdom*, are given by the Holy Spirit in moments when natural insight and human wisdom come to the end of themselves. God has given us common sense, but that's just it, it's common. There are times when heaven's perspective is needed, and the Holy Spirit intervenes supernaturally beyond our natural thinking with a word from heaven for the moment. A specific word for a specific moment, with a specific purpose, supernaturally imparted by the Holy Spirit. *Faith* is part of our Christian experience, but there are times when we face challenges which, naturally speaking, seem impossibly daunting or insurmountable. They require resources which don't seem to exist and change which seems impossible. In these moments, supernaturally the Holy Spirit elevates our faith, we surprise ourselves by the level of faith we feel, all doubts are vanquished, the possibility of failure is banished, and dropped into our hearts is an overwhelming confidence that our God will bring His eternal purposes to pass.

The *healing gifts* are the outworking of God's healing power in bringing complete health and wholeness supernaturally to those who are sick and diseased. They are His healing gifts, plural: the healing of bodies, healing of minds, inner healing, healing of relationships, healing of disease. Always remember, though, that miraculous healing can be conditional upon confession and forgiveness. Jesus often healed in response to faith. Healing gifts are accompanied by the *working of miracles*. A miracle is an amazing and astonishing supernatural event, when God steps in, natural laws are held in abeyance and confounded, and God's creative power intervenes to bring about a change that cannot be explained rationally, logically or scientifically. Natural laws are defied as supernatural intervention takes over. However, supernatural phenomena are never given simply for the purpose of amazing, astounding, amusing or entertaining, but to reveal the power of God at work.

The gift of *prophecy* is when the Holy Spirit comes upon someone and speaks through them a word from God for the moment. Paul says it 'is for strengthening, encouragement and comfort'. While prophecy is revelation, and makes the mind of God clear to the recipients, it must never be exalted to the level of biblical revelation. Prophecy may help illuminate Scripture, but it can never replace it. Prophecies are to be weighed and

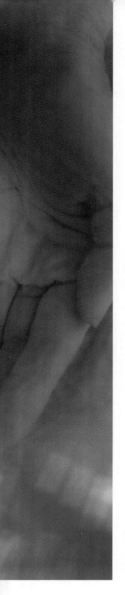

judged, but not taken lightly. 'Do not … treat prophecies with contempt' (1 Thess. 5:20). Some people misinterpret the *discerning of spirits*, and describe this gift as a spirit of discernment, but this gift refers to the supernatural awareness that the Holy Spirit brings to enable us to distinguish whether a manifestation or given response is from the Holy Spirit, the human spirit or a demonic spirit, exposing counterfeits, deceptions and imposters (Acts 16:16–18).

The gift of *tongues and the interpretation of tongues* is probably the most controversial of all the spiritual gifts listed in the New Testament, and has often divided evangelical Christians. It is a supernatural utterance in a tongue never learned by the speaker. Paul underlines that a public use of this gift in a congregation needs to be accompanied by the gift of interpretation of tongues, otherwise it will be meaningless to those who are gathered.

Paul's injunction is to 'earnestly desire the best gifts' (1 Cor. 12:31, NKJV). 'But one and the same Spirit is active in all these, distributing to each one as He wills' (1 Cor. 12:11, HCSB), not to simply enjoy or indulge ourselves in their use, but in order to be *empowered for purpose.*

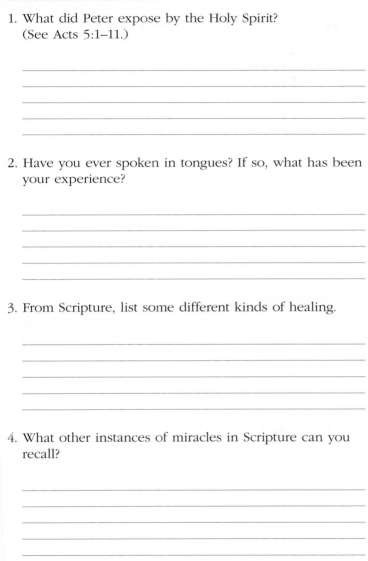

## Discussion Starters

1. What did Peter expose by the Holy Spirit?
   (See Acts 5:1–11.)

   _____

   _____

   _____

   _____

   _____

2. Have you ever spoken in tongues? If so, what has been
   your experience?

   _____

   _____

   _____

   _____

   _____

3. From Scripture, list some different kinds of healing.

   _____

   _____

   _____

   _____

   _____

4. What other instances of miracles in Scripture can you
   recall?

   _____

   _____

   _____

   _____

   _____

5. What is your experience of receiving a word of prophecy?

_____

_____

_____

_____

_____

6. What are your thoughts about Paul's faith on his voyage? (See Acts 27–28.)

_____

_____

_____

_____

_____

## Closing Prayer

Lord, I come afresh to seek Your Holy Spirit and His gifts. You know what is needful in my life, for me to function effectively in Your purposes. Endow me with those gifts that will enable me to serve You well and bring glory to Your name. Amen.

## Final Thought

The Holy Spirit makes available to us both gifts and graces, administered by Him through us, in order to move us from the natural realm of functioning into a supernatural dimension of miracles, signs and wonders. If we are to live the Spirit-filled life, we will need to embrace both the Holy Spirit's gifts and His graces. God has opened up to the Church a doorway into the supernatural through these endowments made available to us. Some Christians veer away from anything to do with the supernatural, because of fear, misunderstanding, unbelief or dispensationalist doctrinal teaching (ie that the gifts of the Spirit were for the building up of the Early Church and have since ceased to be operational). Of course people can go overboard and become fascinated and fixated with the sensational and even the bizarre, but that should not prevent us from seeking the genuine and authentic demonstration of the Spirit's power through the gifts He has made available to the Church. The world has a right to see with its very own eyes the evidence of the works of God so that they might believe (John 20:30–31). Have you received any of the ministry gifts of the Holy Spirit? Why not ask Him for a fresh infilling of the Holy Spirit today?

## Further Study

Joshua 10:13; 2 Kings 6:1–7; Matthew 10:1; Mark 16:17–18; Luke 4:18; Acts 2:4; 5:1–11; 10:46; 15:6–8; 16:16–40; 19:6–11; 21:9; 27; Romans 4:20–21; 8:27; 12:6; 1 Corinthians 2:11–14; 14:1–31; 2 Corinthians 11:13–15; Galatians 3:5; Ephesians 2:8–10; Hebrews 2:1–4; 11:33; James 5:13–20; 1 Timothy 4:14; 1 John 4:1–13.

# A Spirit-filled People ...
*Empowered for Purpose*

## Icebreaker

Identify five different symbols of the Holy Spirit in Scripture and five distinct titles that are applied to the Holy Spirit. Give the scriptural reasons and references for your choices.

## Opening Prayer

Come, Holy Spirit, I not only long to see You working more deeply in my life, but also in Your Church. As I come to this last session of my studies, I am grateful for all You have shown me during this Lent season. I long to live a Spirit-filled life, *empowered for purpose*. I have come too far to turn back now. Flow in, so that Your life and power may flow out, in my home, my work and in my church. Everywhere, Lord, grant that out of my innermost being, day by day, the rivers of living water will flow through me to this needy world. Amen.

## Bible Readings

### Acts 1:1-4

In my former book, Theophilus, I wrote about all that Jesus began to do and to teach until the day he was taken up to heaven, after giving instructions through the Holy Spirit to the apostles he had chosen. After his suffering, he showed himself to these men and gave many convincing proofs that he was alive. He appeared to them over a period of forty days and spoke about the kingdom of God. On one occasion, while he was eating with them, he gave them this command: 'Do not leave Jerusalem, but wait for the gift my Father promised, which you have heard me speak about.'

### Acts 2:43-47

Everyone was filled with awe, and many wonders and miraculous signs were done by the apostles.

All the believers were together and had everything
in common. Selling their possessions and goods,
they gave to anyone as he had need. Every day they
continued to meet together in the temple courts. They
broke bread in their homes and ate together with
glad and sincere hearts, praising God and enjoying
the favour of all the people. And the Lord added to
their number daily those who were being saved.

**Acts 8:15**
When they arrived, they prayed for them that they
might receive the Holy Spirit ...

## Eye Opener

Pentecost (Acts 2:1–4) is recognised by many as the
official birthday of the Church, when the Holy Spirit
descended in the 'upper room' (Acts 1:13, AV), and my,
what celebrations took place. That day, the power of God
was poured out in the Person of the Holy Spirit. The
Church was unleashed into the world, and immediately
amazing things began to happen. The world would never
be the same again. Crowds of onlookers were astonished
and amazed, asking each other, 'What does all this
mean?' (Acts 2:12, CEV). The Spirit-filled Church had
arrived. A place and a people through which amazing and
astonishing signs and wonders were happening. We might
ask ourselves also, what does all this mean for me?

## Setting the Scene

The apostle Paul uses a descriptive phrase when he
gives the benedictory statement in his letter to the
church in Corinth: 'The grace of the Lord Jesus Christ,
and the love of God, and the communion of the Holy
Spirit be with you all' (2 Cor. 13:14, NKJV). We often use
this benediction today. You see, the Church is to be a
communion and community of the Holy Spirit, bestowed
with grace (God's favour), flowing in the abundance of

the love of God. The word 'communion' here means 'partnership with' or 'in participation with'. It carries the idea of being together, working together and journeying together. The Holy Spirit wants to empower us as His partners in ministry, participating with Him to bring the purposes of God to pass in this day and generation. Through communion with the Holy Spirit, we receive the blessing of His supernatural working in us and through us.

Part of the Holy Spirit's work of empowerment is through His deep communion and fellowship with us, where He invites us to be partakers of all the gifts, graces and endowments He bestows. This is described by Paul as 'the supply of the Spirit' (Phil. 1:19, AV). The Greek word describing this aspect of His ministry is *parakletos*, meaning 'one who comes alongside'. Jesus told us that the Holy Spirit would powerfully come alongside as the Divine Paraclete in a number of ways. 'The Father ... shall give you another Comforter ...' (John 14:16, AV) – *comfort*. 'I pray that ... he may strengthen you with power through his Spirit ...' (Eph. 3:16) – *strength*. 'Unless I go away, the Counsellor will not come to you; but if I go, I will send him to you' (John 16:7) – *counsel*. 'He will guide you into all truth' (John 16:13) – *guidance*. What a partnership to be in communion with the Holy Spirit. Truly we will be a Spirit-filled people, *empowered for purpose*.

## A Spirit-filled People

What, then, is a Spirit-filled Church? The answer is Spirit-filled people. Paul describes the Church as a living, loving, liberated body of people. Not a collection of old bones neatly laid out in some religious museum, but a vibrant, energised, dynamic expression, made alive by the breath of the Holy Spirit. A people called out and called together in partnership with God's Spirit for a purpose. Following the Holy Spirit's descent, '... many wonders and miraculous signs were done by the apostles. All the believers were together and had everything in common

... And the Lord added to their number daily those who were being saved' (Acts 2:43–44,47).

Some years later, when Paul arrived at Ephesus and found about a dozen men, the first question he asked them was, 'Did you receive the Holy Spirit when you believed?' (Acts 19:2). I guess it is the same question that he would ask of us today. You cannot partner with someone who isn't with you. 'No,' replied the men, 'we have not even heard that there is a Holy Spirit' (v.2). God never intended His Church to be 'Holy Spiritless', relying on human methods and clever words. 'My speech and my preaching was not with enticing words of man's wisdom, but in demonstration of the Spirit and of power ...'
(1 Cor. 2:4, AV). God has appointed the Holy Spirit to empower, energise and equip His people to continue the work of Jesus Christ in this world. That's what happened at Pentecost, when the Church was born, and any converts who subsequently had not received the Holy Spirit were regarded as lacking the vital necessity of the Holy Spirit's *empowering for purpose.*

As 120 gathered in an upper room that day, the Spirit came like a mighty rushing wind from heaven, filling and thrilling the gathered disciples. Supernatural phenomena followed: wind, fire, speaking in tongues, powerful preaching, thousands saved, with miraculous signs and wonders. These were extraordinary events marking the outpouring of the Holy Spirit, but no place was given to foolishness, extravagance or self-indulgence. Why? Because 'they continued stedfastly in the apostles' doctrine and fellowship' (Acts 2:42, AV). The Word of God was the anchor holding them steady, stabilised and focused. The living Word, the Lord Jesus, was proclaimed, the written Word, the sacred Scripture, was explained, with the spoken word, their testimony, exclaimed. The Holy Spirit would teach and remind them of all that Jesus had said and done. As Donald Gee, a saint of yesteryear, once said, 'All Word and you dry up, all Spirit and you blow up, but with the Word and the Spirit you grow up'.

Jesus said that the work of the Spirit would be to glorify Him (John 16:13–14). This happened immediately as Peter lifted Jesus' name high in the marketplace: 'We are witnesses of these things, and so is the Holy Spirit, whom God has given to those who obey him' (Acts 5:32). Directly following the outpouring of God's Spirit upon them, they became outwardly focused. Their hearts turned to the practical matters of caring for each other, sacrificing their own assets and meeting the needs of their community: 'All the believers were together and had everything in common. Selling their possessions and goods, they gave to anyone as he had need' (Acts 2:44–45). When the Holy Spirit moves, there is not only an inflow but an outworking. This was the Holy Spirit partnering with hungry and available people. These are the 'unforced rhythms of grace' (Matt. 11:29, *The Message*) of the Spirit-filled life, outgoing, creative, practical, connecting, giving, contributing and serving others. When our hearts open inwardly to receive, they turn outwardly to demonstrate the love of Christ to a needy world. God will never stop giving as long as we are willing to receive. He has called us to be a people of power – His power – *empowered for purpose*: '... because our gospel came to you not simply with words, but also with power, with the Holy Spirit ...' (1 Thess. 1:5).

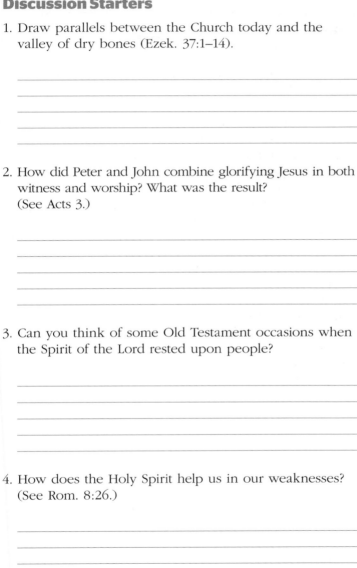

## Discussion Starters

1. Draw parallels between the Church today and the valley of dry bones (Ezek. 37:1–14).

2. How did Peter and John combine glorifying Jesus in both witness and worship? What was the result?
   (See Acts 3.)

3. Can you think of some Old Testament occasions when the Spirit of the Lord rested upon people?

4. How does the Holy Spirit help us in our weaknesses?
   (See Rom. 8:26.)

5. How do we receive the three aspects of the Word, living, written and spoken?

_____

_____

_____

_____

_____

6. What do you think it meant to the Christians to have 'everything in common' (Acts 2:44)?

_____

_____

_____

_____

_____

7. In what ways do we function 'in the energy of the flesh' (Gal. 3:3, RSV)?

_____

_____

_____

_____

_____

## Closing Prayer

Lord, I recognise I need a daily, moment by moment dependency on Your Holy Spirit's power flowing through me and out of me. Help me to drink daily the water of Your Spirit, so that as You pour in, I might pour out to bless others. Amen.

## Final Thought

We have seen throughout these studies that the Spirit-filled atmosphere of the New Testament Church was nothing short of powerfully dynamic. J.B. Phillips, when translating the book of Acts, said that he felt like an electrician working in an old house where the wires were still alive and the sparks were still flying. Let's be clear, the Spirit-filled Church is not a club for analysts and researchers, or a classroom for students of prophecy. It is a dynamic, vibrant body of people *empowered for purpose*, reaching out to the lost and needy with the redeeming grace of Jesus Christ in the power of the Holy Spirit. Paul declared, 'But if ... an unbeliever ... enters, he is convicted ... the secrets of his heart are disclosed, and so, falling on his face, he will worship God and declare that God is really among you' (1 Cor. 14:24–25, ESV). If we are to be a Spirit-filled people, we again need to embrace a gospel that includes miracles, signs and wonders, fulfilling the great commission to 'Go into all the world and preach the gospel ... And these signs will follow those who believe ...' (Mark 16:15–17, NKJV).

## Further Study

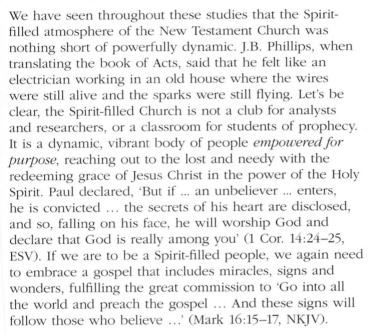

Judges 6:34; 14:19; Matthew 10:8; John 4:1–26; 7:37–44; 14:15–31; 15:26; Acts 2:1–3:1–10; 5:12–32; 16:25; 18:11; 20:35; Romans 8:14,26; 1 Corinthians 2:13; 3:5–16; 2 Corinthians 2:12; 9:6–8; Ephesians 4:1–13; 5:22–33.

# Leader's Notes

## Study One: Passion ... Power ... Purpose ...
*Endued from On High*

### Icebreaker
Take a bag of M&Ms and ask everyone to take a handful. Assign a different meaning to each colour, eg red – family; green – school; yellow – occupation etc. As many sweets a group member has in his hands, that is how many facts he is to tell. Each participant may eat the sweets directly after he shares his facts or the whole group can eat the sweets together after the game.

### Discussion Starters
As you work through the questions, invite responses, ensuring that everyone is given the opportunity to contribute if they wish to.

1. Repentance is an act of the will and a decision of the mind. If there is no desire for change, there will be no commitment to it. Desire is the want to change and repentance the willingness. Repentance is a 180-degree turn to face the opposite direction. Someone has said, 'Repentance is agreeing with God; You're right and I'm wrong'.

2. The New Testament Greek word for repentance is *metanoia*, which means 'a change of attitude, heart and direction'. A desire for change is insufficient unless it is acted upon, differentiating repentance from regret, remorse, reformation, restitution and rehabilitation. Change is not genuine unless there is fruit, and that fruit is changed attitudes, changed actions, changed language and changed lifestyle.

3. Read Romans 6:1–4 and talk about the importance of expressing an inward reality through the outward expression of baptism. Think through the aspect of burial in water and of resurrection to newness of life.

4. You are looking here for the response of abstaining,

or going without something, whether coffee, TV, dessert, newspaper etc, or fasting one or several meals. It is good to think through the idea of monetising the value of what we go without and making it part of the almsgiving of Lent. Think about types of community service that you could connect with during Lent.

5. Look at Acts 2, perhaps in particular the first eighteen verses. In verse 4 we read that the waiting disciples were 'filled with the Holy Spirit'. Note the different impacts the descent of the Spirit had upon them. As the group leader, list the impacts before the session in preparation.

6. Oil is mentioned many times in Scripture, and has always been accepted and recognised as a symbol of the Holy Spirit. The priest was anointed for Temple duties (Lev. 4:1–3; Psa. 133:1–3); the prophet to speak on behalf of God (1 Kings 19:16; Psa. 105:15); and the king to serve the nation through the rule of righteousness (1 Sam. 16:13; Psa. 132:10). These were all practical offices in the carrying out of God's work. After discussing this, talk about what Luke 4:18 means at practical levels.

7. Look at Acts 1:8 and discuss what it means to be witnesses. Then, looking at Acts 2:41–43, talk about the concept of signs and wonders related to witness.

## Study Two: Released in the Spirit ...
*Energised for Life*

### Icebreaker

Energy can mean different things to different people. Things that might come up in the group are: people expending energy in activity such as sport; and the energy of the sun and solar power. Man-made energy sources might be mentioned, such as hydroelectricity; natural fuel sources, including coal, oil and wind; nuclear energy and power; and simpler forms, such as a battery or bicycle dynamo. The important thing is to distinguish between the energy itself – like electricity; the source of the energy – like coal and oil; and the process by which it is created – power station or jet engine; then apply the principle to divine energy.

**Discussion Starters**

1. People have different experiences of and encounters with the Holy Spirit, and it is encouraging to hear them recounted. They may be different and varied but all are valid if they accord with Scripture. If someone shares something that you would not attribute to the Holy Spirit, you will need to gently point this out. The important thing is not to let people impose their experiences on others as the norm for everyone.

2. Again, you may get some particular doctrinal viewpoints depending on people's denominational background or affiliation. Respect them. You may have someone who holds the view that the signs and wonders of the book of Acts were for the Early Church only and not for today. Encourage healthy discussion, with biblical reference as well as personal experience. A good place to start may be 1 Corinthians 13:8–12, which speaks of the gifts of the Spirit being in operation until 'perfection comes', when Jesus returns.

3. Get responses. You are looking for things such as a daily quiet time, times of worship, times of waiting on God etc.

4. Draw out that Paul is warning them not to get drunk because it debilitates and disorientates, whereas the Holy Spirit energises and invigorates. His emphasis is not *don't* get drunk on wine, but *do* get intoxicated with the Spirit. The observers on the Day of Pentecost suggested the disciples were drunk because they were astonished and could find no other explanation. Peter got up and preached. Talk about the content of his sermon. That's what being filled with the Spirit can do.

5. Some people are a little fearful, others don't know what to expect. Take a look at Elisha receiving Elijah's mantle (2 Kings 2:1–18).

6. I could do this for you, but you read them and find out for yourself, and for the group, then you can tell them!

7. Gently draw from the members of the group whether they are experiencing the impact of the Spirit's empowering in their lives for witness, ministry and worship. Use positive testimonies from members, not to make others feel guilty, but to encourage in all a hunger for more of the things of the Spirit. Take the opportunity to pray together and seek the Lord for a fresh infilling. Commence this time with some worship songs inviting the Holy Spirit to come and do a fresh work among you and fill each of you to overflowing.

## Study Three: Growing in the Spirit …
*Enriched in Character*

### Icebreaker
Encourage members of the group to talk about the particular qualities that they find enjoyable, as well as the texture and feel of the fruit. For instance, some people like soft juicy sweet fruits, while others like firm tart flavours.

### Discussion Starters
1. Draw out that these things listed are not isolated and disparate, but all fruit from the same tree and come as a whole. Some suggest that love is the fruit and everything that follows is an expression and outworking of it. Have you ever seen a young couple madly in love? What do they exude? It's joy. Explore the rest of the fruit of the Spirit in this way with the group.

2. Reflect on this definition of love and ask for responses to it. Illustrate it in biblical context by inserting it into a Scripture verse in place of the word 'love'. For example, use John 3:16 or Hebrews 12:6. Invite other definitions of love from the group.

3. Point out how the Samaritan was other-centred, and the Levi and priest self-centred. Draw out and identify the different things the Samaritan did for the wounded man – there are around ten. Highlight the issue between Jews and Samaritans, and draw out the fact that Jesus never called the Samaritan a *good* Samaritan, he was just an ordinary one showing extraordinary love and care.

4. Open up the whole area of the fruit of the Spirit being evidenced in our lives. Ask the group to come up with ideas of practical outworkings. For example, self-control is not speeding, not comfort eating, not being sarcastic etc. This behaviour is not achieved through superhuman effort, but by a work of the fullness of the Spirit in our lives. If these things are a continual struggle to us, it is a sure sign that we need a fresh infilling of the Holy Spirit.

5. The key thing to bring out is that when we are deeply loved, we are deeply secure, and it is that security which gives us stability and peace despite our circumstances. The thing to bring out is not that the Lord has peace that He dispenses as soon as we hit a storm, but that God is love, and therefore peace is a dimension of the essence of His character. That is why Jesus is the Prince of Peace (Isa. 9:6). As we are hid in Him in the cleft of the rock, He is our peace. Even before we hit the storm, He is our peace, and it is that peace which continues during the storm and after it, as we are held securely in His love.

6. Biblical examples you could look at are: Job (book of Job), Hannah (1 Sam. 1:9–19); Paul and Silas (Acts 16:22–26). Also look at Abraham, who lost patience and took things into his own hands – with dire consequences (Gen. 16). Encourage personal testimony of how people have handled adversity.

7. Explore the idea that longsuffering is retaining an active interest and willingness to engage, support and sacrifice in an ongoing way, whereas indifference withdraws, shrugs its shoulders, and takes the attitude 'You can stew in your own juice'.

## Study Four: The Third Dimension ...
*Enlightened Within*

### Icebreaker

You are looking here to explore what a person feels *they* would want to do, not what someone else can make happen or something that is a grand gesture, such as feeding all the hungry. You are looking to discover what their level of personal engagement would be, if it could be made possible somehow.

### Discussion Starters

1. For characteristics of the spirit, you might want to consider conscience, spiritual sensitivity, motivations, spiritual insight, the 'God vacuum'; for the soul, the intellect, the emotions, the will; the body, the five physical senses.

2. A complete and fulfilled life depends on the proper balance of spirit, soul and body. This determines the relationship in our spiritual world, psychological world and physical world. It was God's intention that the spirit, made alive to Him, would be the dominant part of the personality, with the psychological and physical drives being subservient to it. When this happens, freedom and harmony in the personality is enjoyed.

3. If a large group, break up into three smaller groups, dividing between you the list of fifteen acts of the sinful nature. Consider how we might easily slip into them. For example, taking sexual immorality, you could look at the words of Jesus in the Sermon on the Mount, which explain that we can commit adultery in our hearts (Matt. 5:27–28). Without deliberately setting out to, we can slip into adultery through looking at inappropriate material on the internet, at page three girls, at some TV and movies etc.

4. Use your concordance to find the references. You are looking for things like weak, defiled, seared, dulled, evil, pure, good, void of offence. Discuss what these verses imply about the conscience.

5. As we allow the Holy Spirit to fill us there becomes a heightened awareness of what is unrighteous. By responding to the Spirit's promptings He provides us with power to turn away, walking in the paths of righteousness. We do not have to give in to sin in order to be aware of the conviction of the Spirit, but when He fills us we become far more sensitive to what is unrighteous.

6. Consider Paul's admonition in verses 22–24 to 'put off' the old self and 'put on' the new self. We need to recognise old patterns of thinking we may not have discarded, and embrace new patterns of thought revealed in God's Word. Using Discussion Starter 1, look at the contrasts Paul highlights in verses 25–29, listing what he exhorts us to 'put off' and 'put on' in relation to the spirit, soul and body. Identify some of the life patterns that go with these things. Begin to explore the idea of taking thoughts captive (see 2 Cor. 10:5), drawing out the point that when someone is taken captive it is usually with an amount of effort or force. Taking captive carries the idea of active pursuit not compliant surrender.

## Study Five: The Giver of Gifts ...
*Equipped to Serve*

### Icebreaker
Wrap some simple gifts, eg a chocolate bar, a bar of soap, some things from the £1 shop. The gifts do not need to be expensive or extravagant. Put them in a bowl and pass the bowl around. Ask people to say what they think of their gifts, and if there is a gift someone else has which they would prefer.

### Discussion Starters
1. Read the account in Acts 5:1–11 and explore what gifts were in operation. Look particularly at verse 3, the aspect of the Holy Spirit exposing the lie and Peter confronting the deceit by exposing it with a greatly

accurate word of knowledge. Then look at Peter's conversation with Sapphira, particularly the statement, 'How could you agree to test the Spirit of the Lord' (v.9). Talk about the effect on the Church – 'great fear seized the whole church' (v.11) – and think about the resulting conviction of the Holy Spirit.

2. This question may well provoke some lively discussion. Let people express their own experiences, but don't allow anyone to impose his or her experience on others. The gift of tongues is often described as a supernatural prayer language. You may feel it appropriate to pray together for those who have not received an infilling of the Holy Spirit. You may also want to explore the aspect of singing in the Spirit.

3. Talk about physical healing and give examples from the Gospels and the book of Acts, eg the blind man, the leper, the woman with an issue of blood, the lame man etc. Look up these passages in preparation. Look up passages about forgiveness, such as the story of the prodigal son and Peter questioning Jesus about forgiveness in Matthew 18:15–22. For inner healing, Luke 13:11–17.

4. Recall at least ten miracles from the Old Testament that defy natural laws, like the parting of the Red Sea, the floating axe head, manna in the wilderness etc. Also recall at least ten miracles from the New Testament. Not only identify them but also look up the passages and read the accounts together. You need to take time to research these yourself before your group gathering.

5. Invite members of the group to recount a specific prophetic promise which God has given to them in the past. It may be directly from His Word, through the preached word or through another person. For some, they will have seen the promise fulfilled or being fulfilled, others may still be waiting on the promise for God's timing and circumstance. After sharing, encourage each another and pray together, being open to God speaking further into your life and the lives of those in your group.

6. Read together Acts 27:2–28:10. Think through the

circumstances of Paul's last voyage, as he is taken to be imprisoned at Rome. Despite this being his last journey to prison, he shows great determination not to escape but to arrive at his appointed destination. Explore the aspects of faith that he demonstrated, despite the impossible circumstances of the elements against him. Look at the outcome and the impact on other people's lives.

## Study Six: A Spirit-filled People ...
*Empowered for Purpose*

### Icebreaker
For symbols of the Holy Spirit, you are looking for things like oil, water, wind, fire, dove and breath. For titles or names, Counsellor, Comforter, the Spirit of Truth, the Spirit of Life, The Spirit of Grace, the Spirit of Wisdom and the Eternal Spirit.

### Discussion Starters
1. Explore the idea of dryness and a pile of dry bones in a boneyard. Then that the dry bones rattled and came together, but still only became skeletons in a graveyard. From there they only became corpses in a mass morgue. These are miracles in themselves, but corpses are of no use unless the breath of life comes into them and they become living beings. This is what happened in Ezekiel's valley. Draw parallels with today's Church, with all its programmes, modern whistles and bells, gizmos etc. Are we at the stage of rattling bones, of skeletons, of corpses or of a living body?

2. Read the account in Acts 3, highlighting the fact that this occurred right after Pentecost, when Peter and John were going to the Temple to pray. Being outwardly focused they witnessed to a man in financial and physical need, and literally reached out to him and saw a miracle take place. The man walked and leapt, praising God. As a result, Peter went on to preach Jesus to the crowd.

3. Look up Bible passages in which the following list of people experienced the Spirit of the Lord being upon them: Samson, David, Saul, Isaiah, Joseph, Moses, Joshua, Othniel, Gideon, Jephthah, Samuel etc. Note down any other people you find and share relevant Bible verses with the group.

4. Romans 8:26 is about the intercessory ministry of the Holy Spirit through us. There are times when we don't know what to pray or how to pray. Some believe this verse refers to praying in tongues or 'the Holy Spirit prayer language' as some describe it. That may be. What is certain is that it is referring to being so attuned to the Holy Spirit, who knows the will of God, that when we don't know how to pray He helps us in our weakness.

5. The Living Word is the Lord Jesus, the Divine Logos, whom we receive at salvation. The Word is made flesh in us, as He comes to live and dwell in us. Discuss Colossians 1:27: '... Christ in you, the hope of glory'. The written Word is the sacred text of Scripture; talk about the importance of regularly reading, meditating on and memorising Scripture. Invite members of the group to quote a Bible verse from memory and explain why it is important to them. The spoken Word comes through preaching, and by declaring our testimony to others. The confession of our faith.

6. Having 'everything in common' (Acts 2:44): This is a challenging idea in today's world, where we are taught to be acquisitive and to look after our own interests. It is a counter-intuitive biblical concept. Explore with the group the idea of living in a community which had 'everything in common'. How comfortable would you feel?

7. You are looking for the group to come up with things like: self-reliance, trusting in my own abilities, depending on my own finances, running my life to my own agenda, relying on what I know I can do best. The point is that in themselves these things are not necessarily wrong or bad, but it is when we come to depend on them to hold our lives together, rather than trusting in God and the work of His Spirit, that we get into difficulties. The energy of the flesh eventually burns out, and there is nothing left in the tank.

# National Distributors

**UK: (and countries not listed below)**
CWR, Waverley Abbey House, Waverley Lane, Farnham, Surrey GU9 8EP.
Tel: (01252) 784700 Outside UK (44) 1252 784700 Email: mail@cwr.org.uk

**AUSTRALIA:** KI Entertainment, Unit 21 317-321 Woodpark Road, Smithfield, New South Wales
2164. Tel: 1 800 850 777  Fax: 02 9604 3699 Email: sales@kientertainment.com.au

**CANADA:** David C Cook Distribution Canada, PO Box 98, 55 Woodslee Avenue, Paris,
Ontario N3L 3E5. Tel: 1800 263 2664 Email: swansons@cook.ca

**GHANA:** Challenge Enterprises of Ghana, PO Box 5723, Accra. Tel: (021) 222437/223249
Fax: (021) 226227 Email: ceg@africaonline.com.gh

**HONG KONG:** Cross Communications Ltd, 1/F, 562A Nathan Road, Kowloon.
Tel: 2780 1188 Fax: 2770 6229 Email: cross@crosshk.com

**INDIA:** Crystal Communications, 10-3-18/4/1, East Marredpalli, Secunderabad – 500026, Andhra
Pradesh. Tel/Fax: (040) 27737145 Email: crystal_edwj@rediffmail.com

**KENYA:** Keswick Books and Gifts Ltd, PO Box 10242-00400, Nairobi.
Tel: (254) 20 312639/3870125 Email: keswick@swiftkenya.com

**MALAYSIA:** Canaanland, No. 25 Jalan PJU 1A/41B, NZX Commercial Centre, Ara Jaya, 47301
Petaling Jaya, Selangor. Tel: (03) 7885 0540/1/2 Fax: (03) 7885 0545 Email: info@canaanland.com.my

Salvation Book Centre (M) Sdn Bhd, 23 Jalan SS 2/64, 47300 Petaling Jaya, Selangor.
Tel: (03) 78766411/78766797 Fax: (03) 78757066/78756360
Email: info@salvationbookcentre.com

**NEW ZEALAND:** KI Entertainment, Unit 21 317-321 Woodpark Road, Smithfield,
New South Wales 2164, Australia. Tel: 0 800 850 777 Fax: +612 9604 3699
Email: sales@kientertainment.com.au

**NIGERIA:** FBFM, Helen Baugh House, 96 St Finbarr's College Road, Akoka, Lagos.
Tel: (01) 7747429/4700218/825775/827264 Email: fbfm@hyperia.com

**PHILIPPINES:** OMF Literature Inc, 776 Boni Avenue, Mandaluyong City.
Tel: (02) 531 2183 Fax: (02) 531 1960 Email: gloadlaon@omflit.com

**SINGAPORE:** Alby Commercial Enterprises Pte Ltd, 95 Kallang Avenue #04-00, AIS Industrial
Building, 339420. Tel: (65) 629 27238 Fax: (65) 629 27235 Email: marketing@alby.com.sg

**SOUTH AFRICA:** Struik Christian Books, 80 MacKenzie Street, PO Box 1144, Cape Town 8000.
Tel: (021) 462 4360 Fax: (021) 461 3612 Email: info@struikchristianmedia.co.za

**SRI LANKA:** Christombu Publications (Pvt) Ltd, Bartleet House, 65 Braybrooke Place, Colombo 2.
Tel: (9411) 2421073/2447665 Email: dhanad@bartleet.com

**USA:** David C Cook Distribution Canada, PO Box 98, 55 Woodslee Avenue, Paris, Ontario N3L 3E5,
Canada. Tel: 1800 263 2664 Email: swansons@cook.ca

**CWR is a Registered Charity - Number 294387**
**CWR is a Limited Company registered in England - Registration Number 1990308**

Day and Residential Courses
Counselling Training
Leadership Development
Biblical Study Courses
Regional Seminars
Ministry to Women
Daily Devotionals
Books and DVDs
Conference Centre

# Trusted all Over the World

CWR HAS GAINED A WORLDWIDE reputation as a centre of excellence for Bible-based training and resources. From our headquarters at Waverley Abbey House, Farnham, England, we have been serving God's people for over 40 years with a vision to help apply God's Word to everyday life and relationships. The daily devotional *Every Day with Jesus* is read by nearly a million readers an issue in more than 150 countries, and our unique courses in biblical studies and pastoral care are respected all over the world. Waverley Abbey House provides a conference centre in a tranquil setting.

**For free brochures** on our seminars and courses, conference facilities, or a catalogue of CWR resources, please contact us at the following address:
**CWR, Waverley Abbey House, Waverley Lane, Farnham, Surrey GU9 8EP, UK**

Telephone: **+44 (0)1252 784700**
Email: **mail@cwr.org.uk**
Website: **www.cwr.org.uk**

**CWR** Applying God's Word
*to everyday life and relationships*

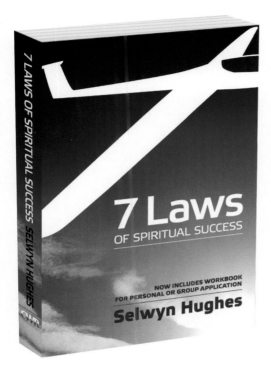

# Discover the basic laws that govern your spiritual life

Many Bible teachers tell us what we should do as Christians but Selwyn Hughes tells us how to do it. This key teaching that Selwyn Hughes considered to be his legacy to future generations will help you to walk in step with the Holy Spirit.

This edition includes probing questions and practical action plans.

**7 Laws of Spiritual Success extended edition**
280-page paperback, 230x153mm
ISBN: 978-1-85345-468-4

**Available online at www.cwr.org.uk/store or call 01252 784710.**

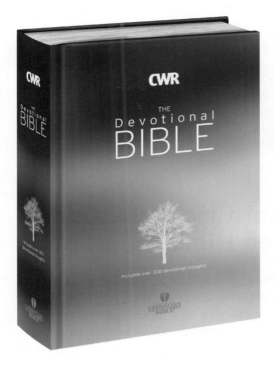

# Wisdom and insights in a hardback Bible

This beautifully presented Bible includes life-changing insights with its selections from CWR's four daily devotionals for adults.

And its meditations on the names of God and profiles of Bible characters, appropriately placed throughout the text, will deepen your understanding.

Makes an ideal gift!

**The Devotional Bible**
1,778-page hardback with ribbon marker, 140x215mm
ISBN: 978-1-85345-527-8

**Available online at www.cwr.org.uk/store or call 01252 784710.**

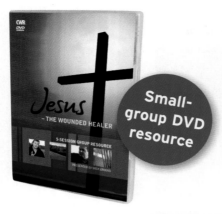

# Draw strength from the God who humbled Himself

There is flesh in the godhead – a face like our face. God has given us Himself and, in becoming a human being, He experienced our weaknesses and much deep suffering. So our God is not impassive or demandingly watching us from a distance. He knows exactly how we feel and He identifies with us in the midst of life's pain and challenges.

These five insightful 15-minute DVD sessions will increase your awareness of God's presence and understanding in the midst of life's trials, and will give you new strength to overcome:

- Loneliness and feeling abandoned by God
- Unjust criticism and misunderstanding
- Pain and suffering
- Grief

and much more.

Presented by Mick Brooks (Chief Executive of CWR) at Wintershall Estate in Surrey with scenes from their famous *Life of Christ* open-air production.

**Jesus - the Wounded Healer DVD**
EAN: 5027957001350
Includes one 48-page personal booklet with discussion questions.
One recommended for each group participant.
**Personal Booklet**
ISBN: 978-1-85345-576-6